WHO KNOWS TE

MOLLY CONE

WHO KNOWS TEN?
Children's Tales of
the Ten Commandments

◆ ◆ ◆ ◆ ◆

Illustrated by Robin Brickman

REVISED EDITION

UAHC Press · New York

Library of Congress Cataloging-in-Publication Data

Cone, Molly.
Who knows ten? : children's tales of the Ten Commandments /
told by Molly Cone ; illustrated by Robin Brickman.—[Rev. ed.]
p.   cm.
Includes bibliographical references.
Summary: Presents each of the Ten Commandments with
stories illustrating their meanings.
ISBN 0-8074-0080-7 (pbk. : alk. paper)
1. Ten commandments—Juvenile literature. 2. Tales.
[1. Ten commandments. 2. Jews—Folklore. 3. Folklore.]
I. Brickman, Robin, ill.   II. Title.
BM520.75.C65 1998
296.3'6—dc21   97-38462
                                CIP
                                AC

To Nathan, Hannah, Sarah, and Samuel

✦　✦　✦

Contents

Acknowledgments

This 1998 revised edition with illustrations by noted artist Robin Brickman introduces *Who Knows Ten?* to a new generation of young readers. Known for her finely detailed drawings, watercolors, and cut and painted paper sculptures, Ms. Brickman brings a colorful and spiritual quality to the stories presented.

My thanks to UAHC Press editor Sharon L. Wechter for her thoughtful help with the revisions made in this new edition and for the source material for the Seventh Commandment story "The Promise," which replaces "The Rabbi's Eye."

The idea for this book was originally suggested to me by Rabbi Alexander M. Schindler when he was director of Education, Commission on Jewish Education, UAHC. The writing was an absorbing task, and I extend my thanks to Jeanette Schrieber, who helped me research and explore the many facets of the stories. Others who contributed their special knowledge to the realization of this book are Rabbi Daniel J. Silver, Rabbi David I. Cedarbaum, Alan D. Bennett,

Ruth Gruber, Sylvia Goldman, and UAHC Press editor Bennett Lovett-Graff and copy editors Kathy Parnass and Annette Abramson.

"The Reminder" is adapted from "A Servant When He Reigns," page 172, *Folktales of Israel*, © University of Chicago Press.

"A Place Called Kushta" is adapted from a talmudic tale, page 398, *A Rabbinic Anthology*, C.G. Montefiore and H. Loewe, © The World Publishing Company.

"The Sweetest Sound" is adapted from "What Melody Is the Sweetest?" page 172, *Folktales of Israel*, © University of Chicago Press.

"The Promise" is adapted from *Songs of Songs Rabbah* 1:4.

"The Reward" and "The Gossip" are adapted from folktales of Jewish origin.

"The Peach, the Pitcher, and the Fur Coat" is adapted in part from "Anatomy of Leadership," page 147, *The Jewish Caravan*, © Leo W. Schwarz, 1935.

What's Inside?

Once, in a puzzle store, I found a little box. Inside it there was another box and inside that another. Each box was complete, each was perfect, and each was different in size and color from the one before.

In this book you will find the Ten Commandments. If you look into the meaning of each commandment, you will find another meaning. And if you look inside that, you may find still another—and so on.

Like the box inside the box in the puzzle store, there is meaning inside meaning in each commandment. And it is strange how many people have looked at the Ten Commandments and yet have never discovered the meanings in them.

In a way, this book is a puzzle book. It gives you a chance to find for yourself the many meanings inside each commandment. Each chapter tells you a story, and each story gives you a truth. Each truth holds inside it something else, which perhaps you never thought of before.

But the story doesn't end there. If you think about it, you will see that what it says has something to do with what is happening every day around you—in your home, your school, and your neighborhood. The way to discover how far the story goes is to talk about the ideas in it with your teacher and your classmates, as well as with your friends and your family.

You will find that many of these ideas are the very issues that people everywhere in the world are talking about today. Talking with people about them and hearing what other people think will help you to think, too.

And when you have come to the end of the stories in this book …

And thus have discovered many of the meanings inside the meanings inside the commandments …

You will know

SOMETHING IMPORTANT.

You will know how to do justice and what is good. And by living that way, you will help to make a world of people who respect and understand one another.

Molly Cone

Who Will Hear?

Long ago, the story is told, a Great Voice rose from a mountaintop and called out to all the nations of people on the earth.

"Who will hear?" the Great Voice asked.

At the sound, it is said, no bird sang, no ox lowed, the ocean did not roar, and no creature stirred.

In the breathless silence, all the peoples of the world listened to the words of the Ten Commandments.

However, as it is told, although all the nations of the world listened, they did not hear. For not one of them wanted to change its way of life to follow God's words.

Not one of them, that is, except a wandering band of people who were not a nation at all. They were slaves who had come from the land of Egypt. They were the Israelites who had once lived in the land of Canaan. When famine struck, they had moved to the land of Egypt. There they lived for many years in peace and plenty, until a cruel Pharaoh made slaves of all the Israelites in his country.

Moses led them out of slavery. He led them out of the land of Egypt into the wilderness, in search of freedom.

There, in the middle of the desert, at the foot of the mountain of Sinai, the wandering people heard the thunder and saw the fire and the smoke. Moses scratched into two tablets of stone the words God called out to all the peoples of the world.

"WHO WILL HEAR?" the Great Voice had asked. The Israelites listened. And they heard …

WHO KNOWS TEN?

· I ·

I Am Your God
Who Took You Out
of the Land of Egypt,
Out of the House
of Slavery

· 1 ·

I Am Your God...

With their ears, the Israelites heard the voice of Moses reading from the tablets of stone. But with their hearts, they were hearing the words of God. They crowded around Moses and the tablets he held.

They were free, the First Commandment said. Hearing this, the Israelites thought they could forget they had lived as slaves in Egypt. The thin trees on the mountainside began to shake with their shouts of joy.

The loud uproar seemed to turn the words on the tablets of stone to fire. The Israelites stopped shouting. They stepped back and shielded their eyes with their hands. But they couldn't seem to shut out the flames. In silence, the people stared through their fingers at the words of the First Commandment.

Then they began to understand what the commandment was really saying. God gave life, it said, and with it God also gave freedom. Life and freedom were part of the same commandment. God meant them to go together.

"Oh!" said the Israelites. They took their hands away from their eyes and looked at one another. What the First Commandment was really saying was that every person God created had the same right to freedom.

"It means we must never take freedom for ourselves alone," one of the wanderers said.

The Israelites nodded. They remembered how they had lived as slaves in Egypt. They remembered—and they promised themselves never to forget.

THE FIRST COMMANDMENT

The Reminder

In a certain kingdom long ago, the people followed a strange custom. When a king died, a royal bird was sent out. The bird flew around, and the person on whose head the bird came to rest was named king. That's the way the king was chosen in this kingdom.

One time a very curious thing happened.

In this kingdom there was a slave who made the fine people of the court laugh, even though his face was sad. They thought he was so funny that they dressed him in a cap of chicken feathers and a belt made of lambs' hooves and gave him a little drum to beat.

One night the slave dreamed that a small voice whispered to him.

He sat up and tried to remember what the voice had said. But all that came to his head was the soft sound—*seeeeds*.

"Seeds? How strange," he thought. "What could it mean?" All the next day he puzzled over the strange dream. He could not make any sense of it.

That evening, as he was putting on his hat of chicken feathers, he saw that a number of small seeds had stuck to his feet. Quickly he scooped them up and because he didn't know what to do with them, he put them into the crown of his hat. Then he ran upstairs to make the people laugh.

But the people of the court did not laugh at him that night. They did not feel like laughing, not even at the funny slave, for their king was dead.

The sad-faced slave crept around behind the king's empty chair and fell asleep. He slept sitting up, with his elbows on his knees and his chin in his hands. And he didn't wake up until he heard a curious sound in the air.

Rubbing his eyes, he peered around. He saw a great bird flying through the castle halls.

He opened his eyes wide for he had never seen a bird like this before. It was so large that the flapping of its wings sent a breeze through the castle rooms.

The bird flew around the room once. It came so close it almost touched the slave. Hastily he pulled out of the way. Then, on hands and knees behind the king's empty chair, he looked out again.

The bird flew around the room a second time. The slave crawled out a bit to see it better.

The bird flew around the room a third time—and landed on the head of the slave.

"Ouch!" said he, trying to push it off. "Shoo! Get away from me!" But the bird sitting on his cap of chicken feathers had found the seeds. It sat there and pecked at them greedily.

A great cry arose from the people. "The king!" they shouted. "The king!"

Suddenly the slave felt many hands upon him. He was lifted high and placed on the king's throne.

"Long live the king!" the ladies and gentlemen of the court shouted, and they all bowed low before him.

"Me?" stuttered the slave. "But I am only a slave!"

They paid no attention to what he said. For the great bird was sitting calmly on his cap of feathers, like an eagle on its nest.

"O King!" said the minister. "You have been chosen by the royal bird. You will rule over our land for the rest of your life. But you must promise one thing."

"What is that?" asked the astonished slave.

"You must never forget that you are king!"

The new king slowly nodded, and the people clapped. The trumpets blew, and everyone shouted.

The king who had been a slave sat up on his high throne, but his face was still sad.

"Build me a hut," he said without a smile. "Build it right outside the palace door."

Puzzled, the minister ordered a small house to be built just outside the great palace door.

The king directed the workmen to make it a simple hut. It was made of rough wood and had no windows. The door was a stout one, however, and on it the king himself placed a huge lock.

The people of the court walked back and forth, looking at the hut curiously. When it was ready, the new king entered it. He stayed only a few minutes. When he came out, he locked the door behind him.

Every year this king issued new laws. One year he decreed that every slave should be set free after working six years. Another year he decreed that slaves should be paid for the work they did and that they could buy their freedom from their masters with the money they earned. One day the king quietly decreed that in this particular kingdom, no one had the right to own someone else. All who lived there were free; there were no more slaves. And the king's face was no longer sad. More and more, the people saw him smile.

But so gradually did these changes come about that the people of his kingdom hardly noticed.

What they did notice was the king's custom of going into the little hut once every year.

One day the minister asked, "What are you guarding so closely in that little house?"

"Inside are my most treasured possessions," the king said. "See for yourself." He unlocked the door and stepped aside.

With great eagerness the minister went into the tiny hut. He came out again, shaking his head. "But I see only a feather cap, a belt of lambs' hooves, and a drum!"

"That's right," the king said, smiling. "I made a promise to you that I would never forget I was king. But at the same time, I made a promise to God that I would never forget I was once a slave."

And after carefully locking the door of the little hut, he went back into his palace.

· II ·

You Shall Have
No Other Gods
Besides Me

· 2 ·

You Shall Have No Other
Gods Besides Me

At the words of the Second Commandment, the Israelites covered their heads with their arms. What they saw was lightning, and what they heard was thunder. But they were not sure and were afraid.

Was the fire God? They wondered. Or was God part of the great sound? Was God in the smoke that poured from the mountaintop?

Where was God? They tried to find a face in the sky, but all they could see was the smoke, the fire, the clouds, and the lightning.

Uneasily the Israelites began to murmur. If they could not see God, how would they know God? Where would they find God?

An old man lifted up his voice: "Hear, O Israel, *Adonai* is our God, and *Adonai* is One."

The Israelites bent their heads and tried to think about the commandment and about God. Instead they thought about themselves and about their freedom and their joy.

"We must think about God," they told themselves firmly. And thinking about God led them to thinking about others.

Quickly each person looked up and around. In every face all saw the same wonder. Thinking of others they each felt closer to God.

That was when they found the answer to their question. Suddenly they knew how they could see God.

THE SECOND COMMANDMENT

The Princess Who Wanted to See God

Once there was a princess who had never cried. She had never had anything to cry about. Whatever in the world she wanted she got. One day she woke up and said that she wanted to see God.

"God?" shouted her father. "You mean GOD? Don't be silly, child. No one in the whole world has seen God."

Princess Eleanor smiled a sweet smile. "That is exactly why I want to see God," she said.

Her father threw up his hands. Although he was often impatient with his only daughter, he loved her very much. He knew that in the end he would do anything she asked of him. And Princess Eleanor knew it, too.

The king called in his Chief of Law and Order.

"My daughter wants to see God," he said. "I order you to take care of it."

The Chief of Law and Order nodded and smiled. He knew very

well who God was, as far as he was concerned. He had no doubt that he could make the little princess see God, too.

So he led the princess to the highest tower in the palace. He showed her the great book of the land, which listed all the laws the people in that kingdom must live by and all the punishments for those who disobeyed.

Solemnly he said, "Look at all the laws in this book, and you will see God."

The king's daughter pushed the great book onto the floor.

"The law is *not* God!" she said, and she stamped her foot. "I want to see God!"

"Bah!" said the Chief of Law and Order, and he went off to tell the king that his daughter was rude and willful.

So the king called his Chief of the Treasury. He was in charge of all the gold in the kingdom.

"My daughter wants to see God," said the king. "I order you to take care of it."

The Chief of the Treasury nodded and smiled. For he knew very well who God was, as far as he was concerned. He had no doubt that he could make the little princess see God, too.

He led the princess down to the deepest dungeon of the castle. There he took out a big key and unlocked a thick door. As the big door swung open, the glitter of the gold inside made the princess blink.

Solemnly the treasurer said, "Look at all the gold in this room, and you will see God."

"But I want to *see* God!" The princess stamped her foot. "Not just a lot of old money!"

The treasurer looked at her flushed cheeks and laid a dry hand on her forehead. Then he hurried off to the king to tell him that the princess must certainly be suffering from a strange kind of sickness.

Because neither of his two chiefs had been able to handle the job, the king decided to do it himself. He began to look around for God.

Thinking about it, it occurred to the king that he didn't know what God looked like. Of course, he had never before bothered to look for God. So he looked in the royal corners, under the royal bed, and even down in the royal kitchen. But he couldn't find God anywhere in the palace.

At last he went out through the palace gates and trudged down the road to the village. On the way he looked up into the trees, around the hedges, and under the rocks. He looked everywhere. But since he was not sure exactly what he was looking for, he didn't find anything.

Soon he came to an old man who was planting a pear tree. The man was so old that he hardly had a breath left in his body, yet he was planting a tree. The king smiled as he sat down to rest a moment.

"Old man," he said, chuckling a little, "do you expect to live long enough to eat the fruits of that tree?"

The old man looked up at the king and then looked down at the deep hole he had dug.

"No," he answered slowly, "but I expect my children will. If not them, their children will." He looked proudly at his handiwork. "Oh,

it will surely be a fine tree some day," he said happily. "God willing, that is."

The king looked at him curiously. "Say, old man, do you know God?"

Now the old man turned to look at him. "Of course," he said. "Don't you?"

The king stroked his royal chin. "I'm really not sure. But my daughter wants more than anything in the world to see God. Can you show God to her?"

The old man straightened up. He had often heard of the little princess who had never cried. He looked up the road toward the palace. Then he looked down the road to a little house close to the road.

"Maybe I can," he said thoughtfully.

When the king brought the old man before the princess, she looked at him suspiciously.

"Have you ever really seen God, old man?" she asked.

The old man nodded, smiling a little.

"Then show God to me!" she ordered in a hard little voice, for she didn't believe he had at all.

"First, you must do something for me," the old man said.

"What do you mean?" said the princess. "What do I have to do?"

"You will only have to come with me to visit someone you don't know."

"Then will you show me God?"

The old man nodded. "If God wills it, I will."

"And if God doesn't," she warned, "you'll be sorry!"

She followed the old man out of the palace, down the road, and in the direction of the village. But they did not go all the way. They stopped at a small house close to the road.

The old man sat down on a box in the yard. "Go in," he said.

The princess looked at him in surprise. She had never been in a place as poor as this before. Timidly she pushed open the door and stepped in.

A girl sat in a chair at the table. Although her smile was bright, her face was quite dirty.

"I am Princess Eleanor," the princess said a little haughtily, and she wrinkled her nose at the smell of something cooking on the stove.

The girl only looked at her. She did not move.

"You're supposed to get up and bow when you meet a princess!" the princess said.

The girl's smile slipped off her face. "I can't," she whispered.

"What do you mean, you can't?" the princess demanded, and she frowned. The stifling room was beginning to make her head ache.

The girl pulled at her skirt. She pointed to her legs. "I can't walk," she whispered. "I never could walk—ever."

"Oh!" said Princess Eleanor. She looked at the girl's legs and then quickly looked away. Hastily she stepped outside and closed the door.

Silently she followed the old man back up the road to the palace.

When they reached the palace hall, the old man turned to her.

"Are you ready?" he said.

"Ready? For what?" asked the princess. She had been so busy thinking about the girl that she had forgotten all about herself.

The old man smiled. "You are ready," he said. To the princess's surprise, he put a mirror into her hand.

"Now close your eyes, hold up the mirror, and look deep into your heart."

The princess closed her eyes and held up the mirror. Suddenly tears began to roll down the cheeks of the princess who had never cried. Big, soft, wet tears.

"Why are you crying?" asked the old man.

"I have been selfish all my life," she said, "and I did not know it until I saw that poor girl." She put down the mirror and opened her eyes.

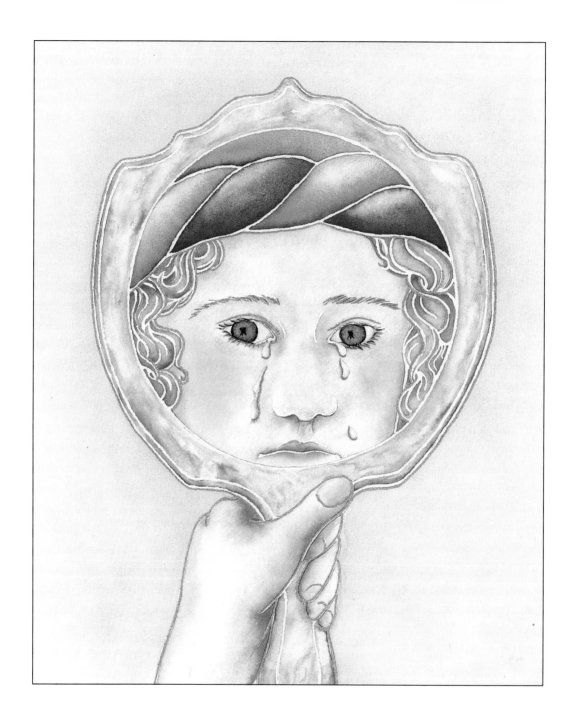

"Oh, sir, do you think it would help if I brought her some food and maybe a pretty dress to wear? Do you think that would help?"

The old man smiled. He took the mirror from her hand and carefully put it away.

"You have seen God," he said.

· III ·

You Shall Not
Use God's Name
Falsely

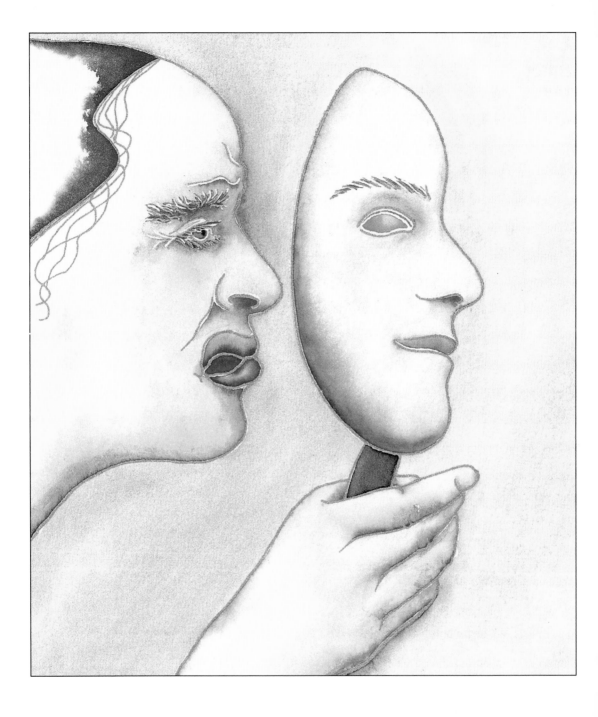

· 3 ·

You Shall Not Use
God's Name Falsely

It was strange how loud the voice of God seemed to the Israelites, even though they heard God only in their hearts. It was so loud that its echo was heard everywhere. The Israelites trembled at the words of the Third Commandment. It is said that the whole world trembled, too.

Although the day was warm and the great flames blazing from the top of the mountain looked hot, many shivered.

Do not use God's name to make a lie seem like the truth, the commandment said. Once your lie is revealed, you will never be trusted again.

The Israelites stood very still, thinking about the Third Commandment. Each one alone pondered the meaning of the words. Then all together they began to understand.

When people do not speak the truth, the world becomes a place in which people cannot trust one another. A world in which people cannot trust one another becomes a world of fear. God was telling them that by breaking a promise to tell the truth, they hurt not only themselves but the whole world.

A murmur arose from the Israelites. They heard the Third Commandment and knew it was a rule not only for themselves but for all people.

THE THIRD COMMANDMENT

A Place Called Kushta

Once there was a town called Kushta. The people who lived there never broke their word, nor did they ever grow old.

Not many of the inhabitants knew why they never grew old. But since they were happy and always kept their word, they had never bothered their heads about it.

One day a king's messenger happened to lose his way and wandered into this little town. He didn't stay long, but he stayed long enough. When he returned to his own country, he brought a most unusual tale to the king.

"In that place no one ever grows old!" he said to the king.

The king's eyes gleamed. Immediately he summoned his wisest counselor.

"In Kushta no one ever grows old," said the king. "Find out why."

Now this counselor knew a great many things. For instance, he knew why apples fell down and why birds flew high. He knew why the earth turned and why the stars blinked. (But he didn't know what would keep the king from growing old.)

"However, I don't mind trying to find out!" he said, and he set out for the town of Kushta.

He walked up and down the streets of Kushta and carefully looked around. All around him he saw ripe golden apricots hanging from the trees. Everywhere he looked, he saw people eating them. The women loaded their aprons with them, the children stuffed their mouths, and the men filled their pockets.

"Aha!" he thought. "*This* must be the reason that no one in Kushta ever grows old."

So he picked a basket full of the ripe fruit. Strapping it carefully to his horse's saddle, he galloped swiftly back to the king.

The king was very pleased when his wise counselor returned with the beautiful apricots. "I will reward you," he said.

But instead of keeping his promise, the king ordered his guards to lock up the counselor. The king certainly didn't intend to let anyone else learn the secret of never growing old.

In his private chamber the king sat down and began to devour the apricots greedily. He ate and he ate, and when he had eaten all the apricots in the basket, he went eagerly to his mirror.

But instead of making him look younger, the apricots seemed to have made him look older and, suddenly, much greener, too! In a rage he smashed the mirror and ordered the faithful counselor put to death.

It wasn't long before the king sent another counselor to Kushta to

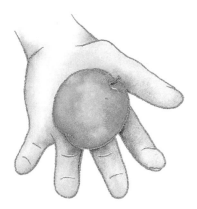

find what it was that kept the people from growing old.

Now the second counselor was even wiser than the first. For instance, he knew why some numbers are round and some square. He knew why clouds made rain and why ice melted. (But he didn't know what would keep the king from growing old.)

"However, I don't mind trying to find out!" he said, and he headed for the town of Kushta. When he reached Kushta, he began searching for the answer to the king's question. He walked up and down the streets of the town and carefully looked around.

All about him were great barrels for catching the rain. Everywhere he looked, he saw people drinking the fresh water from the clouds. The women washed their hair in it; the children bathed in it; the men splashed it on their faces.

"Aha!" he thought. "*This* must be the reason that no one ever grows old here." Quickly he filled a barrel with the rainwater and took it back to the king.

The king was very pleased when the rainwater was brought to him. He ordered it poured into his large tiled tub and promised to reward his counselor immediately. But before taking his rainwater bath, the king secretly ordered his guards to lock up the second counselor, for, of course, the king intended to keep the secret to himself.

He stepped into the tub. But, alas, when he arose again, he was no younger and only a little bit cleaner.

Shaking with anger, as well as with cold, the king ordered the second counselor put to death.

"I will go myself to the place where no one ever grows old," he decided and ordered his carriage. He took with him a sack of gold, and he traveled with great speed.

Reaching the town of Kushta, he headed for the city square. Curious, all the people gathered round.

The king stepped out of the carriage and looked around. Sure enough, no matter where he turned, he saw no person who looked old.

Holding his bag of gold high in the air, he shouted, "A handsome reward for anyone who will tell me what I want to know!"

"What do you want to know?" a young man asked. (He might have been an old man for all the king could tell.)

The king smiled. "Tell me," he said softly, "why the people of Kushta never grow old."

The people looked at one another wide-eyed. Not many of them really knew.

But the king thought they did not trust him. Craftily he raised his right hand and said, "In the name of God, I swear to you, I will reward you handsomely if you tell me your secret."

"It's no secret," one said. "This is the town of truth. That is why it is called Kushta. In our language *kushta* means truth. As long as we live, we always tell the truth." He scratched his head. "I guess that's why we live so long," he said, as though he had not thought about it before.

Everyone nodded. One of them eagerly raised his hands for the bag of gold.

But the secret didn't sound like anything of much value to the king. He pushed the fellow back roughly.

The townsman looked surprised. "The gold!" he said. "You promised to give us a bag of gold!"

But the king was no fool. Why should he give them his gold for nothing? He took his bag of gold and jumped into the carriage. Wildly he whipped his horses home.

But strangely enough, when the carriage reached the palace gates, the king who had broken his word in a place called Kushta was dead.

Something even stranger began to happen in Kushta. The people who had never grown old before suddenly began to grow older.

When the king broke his promise in the town of truth, the spell (if a spell it was) was broken, too. People didn't trust one another completely anymore.

And today, if a traveler should happen to stop in the town called Kushta, he would find it no different from any other place.

· IV ·

Remember the
Sabbath Day
and Keep It Holy

· 4 ·

Remember the Sabbath Day
and Keep It Holy

The Israelites looked at one another, hardly believing their ears. In the Fourth Commandment, God gave them the Sabbath as a day of rest. It was to be their day as well as God's forever.

They were partners with God. They were God's people, the Fourth Commandment told them. Thinking about it, the Israelites stood a little straighter and a little taller.

As free people, the commandment said, they must care about the people around them as well as themselves, and they must care for their families and their animals.

Perhaps the Fourth Commandment, more than any other, gave them hope and gave them courage, for it was more than a reminder, more than a warning, more than a rule. It was a promise. It was a covenant between the Israelites and God. It would be a sign between them forever because it gave them a pattern to follow. It showed them how to live.

The Israelites took the Fourth Commandment most particularly to their hearts. They made it the center of their religion and lived their lives based on it.

THE FOURTH COMMANDMENT

The Sweetest Sound

King Ruben was always asking questions. Every Monday and Thursday he had a new question to ask.

"What is the hottest place in the world?" he wanted to know. "Where is the snow the deepest?" "What is the best month of the year?"

One Thursday he called all his advisers together to ask, "What is the sweetest melody of all?"

The wise men rubbed their chins and looked at one another. They opened their dictionaries and their encyclopedias. They searched through their books of knowledge. Nowhere could they find the answer.

"Why don't you have a contest to find the sweetest melody?" they advised.

So the king called all the musicians in the kingdom to the palace to play their sweetest tunes.

Early in the morning they began to gather under the king's window. They came with flutes and harps and violins, with horns and bells and drums. There were chimes and cymbals and gongs, lutes and lyres and trumpets, and more.

The sounds of their tuning and scraping and testing woke the king at sunrise. Smiling, King Ruben jumped out of his royal bed.

"Each of you in turn will play a tune," he ordered. "When you have all finished, I will decide which melody is the sweetest to my ears."

So they began. All through the morning the king sat on his balcony and listened. By noon he had listened to all the sounds imaginable that could be made by plucking, tinkling, blowing, and banging.

"What do you think?" one adviser asked.

"What do *you* think?" another adviser answered.

Then they cupped their hands around their ears and listened some more.

By the middle of the afternoon, the king had heard all the melodies that could be made by whistling, jingling, and shaking, and by sawing, buzzing, and pounding.

"O King!" said the advisers. "To your ears, which melody is the sweetest?"

King Ruben listened through one ear, then he listened through the other. He listened standing up, and he listened sitting down. He listened with his eyes closed, and he even tried listening with his mouth open.

By late Friday afternoon every sound-making instrument in the whole land had been brought before the king and had played its sweetest tune.

"Hmm," said the king. "Hmmmm," he said again. But he could not tell exactly which sound was the sweetest.

Then the wisest adviser stepped forward. "Why don't you ask all the musicians to play their instruments at the same time? Surely when you hear them all together, the sweetest melody will be found."

The king clapped his hands. "Wonderful!" he said. And he gave the signal for all the instruments in the kingdom to be played at the same time.

The violins sang, the flutes burbled, the harps twanged, the horns blew, the bells rang, the drums pounded, the chimes pealed, the cymbals banged, the gongs rang, the lyres strummed, the trumpets blared, the pipes whistled, the lutes lilted, and all the other instruments rattled and beat and gurgled as sweetly as they could. All together. At the same time.

King Ruben wrinkled up his face and listened with all his might. The advisers covered their ears with their hands and raised their eyes to heaven.

Just at this moment a woman, dressed in her Sabbath best, pushed her way to the front of the crowd.

"O King!" she called at the top of her voice.

The noise was so great that the king could hardly hear her. He leaned over and put his ear close to her mouth.

"I have the answer to your question!" she shouted.

"Eh?" said King Ruben.

"The answer!" she said. "I have it!"

The king looked at her with surprise. She carried no instrument.

"Why didn't you come up before?" he shouted above all the tunes. And he clasped his hands to his head for it was beginning to ache.

The woman said, "If you please, sir, I had to wait until the sun was about to set."

The king looked at the musicians puffing and blowing and pounding and strumming. Sure enough, the sun was low. But there was so much noise, he could no longer hear himself think.

"Stop!" he shouted to all the music makers.

"Stop! Stop!" shouted the advisers.

And just as the sun dipped to the horizon, the sounds of the farthest instruments began to fade away.

"Well?" said King Ruben.

The woman took two candles from her pocket. She placed them on the railing of the balcony. She struck a match. The flames of the candles flickered up just as the sun began to go down. Covering her eyes with her hands, she said, "Blessed are You, *Adonai* our God, Ruler of the universe, who sanctified us by Your commandments and commanded us to kindle the Sabbath lights."

Then she took her hands away from her face. "Those who have ears to hear, let them hear," she said.

The king raised his head. The advisers took their hands away from their ears. The people in the crowd put down their instruments.

"What is it?" whispered the king. He could hear nothing at all.

"It is the sound of rest," the woman said. "Listen and tell me—is not the peace of the Sabbath the sweetest melody of all?"

The king listened; the wise men listened; the people listened. The sound of rest filled the kingdom. At the blessed quiet, King Ruben breathed a sigh of relief.

"Ahhhhhhhh," he said.

"Ahhhhhhhh," echoed all the people.

Then, "Ah!" said the king again. For he had his answer. "The peace of the Sabbath is the sweetest melody of all."

· **V** ·

Honor Your Father
and Your Mother

· 5 ·

Honor Your Father and Your Mother

The voice of Moses grew loud and stern as he read the words of the Fifth Commandment. The words seemed to shine on the tablets of stone.

"Honor is love, honor is respect," the older children explained to the younger ones.

Then even the smallest child knew how important this commandment was. Their parents had told them they must honor God. Now God was telling them to love and respect their parents. It was exactly the same!

Children and parents smiled at one another. Showing that you honor your parents was part of the way you honor God. They all understood that.

The Israelites listened to the Fifth Commandment and remembered Abraham. God had promised Abraham that his people, the Israelites, would be a great nation. But at the same time God had given a warning: "A nation without honor for God will not endure!"

As a nation, they were only beginning. With the Fifth Commandment, God was telling them how to make sure that they would become a great nation that would go on forever.

Thoughtfully they looked again at the glowing words on the tablets of stone. Honor was like a great mirror. Wherever it was held, it reflected back again.

The Israelites nodded. Now they knew exactly what the words meant.

THE FIFTH COMMANDMENT

A Big Red Tomato

Hurrying a little, Mr. Benjamin closed up his grocery store. He could hardly wait to get home. Something very special had happened that day.

But before he went out the door, he picked up the biggest, roundest, most beautiful tomato he could find in the window. Mr. Benjamin smiled as he thought how pleased his mother would be with such a fine tomato.

On his way home, he stopped to see his parents and to leave the tomato, although he did not tell them what had happened. There's no use spoiling a surprise, Mr. Benjamin believed.

He couldn't help grinning as he drove his car into his garage.

"Margaret!" he called to his wife, even before he had opened the kitchen door. "Margaret! It's happened!"

"What's happened?" replied Mrs. Benjamin, but she didn't really have to ask. Somehow she already knew, and she began to smile.

Mr. and Mrs. Benjamin had no children. For a long time they had looked for a baby to adopt. They had written letters, filled out application forms, and taken health tests—and waited. They had waited and waited.

Mr. Benjamin pulled a letter from his pocket. "It has finally come!" he said.

His wife read it. She looked at him doubtfully. "But it doesn't say they have a baby for us. It only says that they want to talk to you."

Mr. Benjamin looked at the letter again. She was right. That was all it said. But he smiled anyway.

"Oh, that's just the way it's written," he said. "What they mean is they have a baby for us if we want it."

"Of course we want it," said Mrs. Benjamin.

"We'll get it all right," Mr. Benjamin said.

But he wasn't quite so sure when he arrived at the adoption office the next day.

"So you want to be a father," Mr. Day said. He looked at the letter Mr. Benjamin showed him.

Mr. Benjamin nodded.

Mr. Day sat down behind his desk. He pressed a button. It made a buzzing sound. The office door opened and a young woman came in.

"The other prospective father is waiting outside," she said.

"You mean there are two babies?" Mr. Benjamin asked.

Mr. Day shook his head. "No, there is only one baby who needs a home. But there are two families who want him."

Feeling uneasy, Mr. Benjamin stood aside as the other man came in. He looks something like me, he thought. It was true. As they stood side by side in front of the desk, they looked very much alike. They were about the same age, with the same color hair. They wore the same kind of clothes, and they were both nervous. I guess he's just as anxious as I am, Mr. Benjamin thought.

"I have called you here for a very important reason," Mr. Day said to them. "I read your applications carefully. They were almost complete, but not quite." Mr. Benjamin wondered what he had left out.

"There is something neither of you mentioned. Something so important that it is of more account than all the fine things each of you has promised to give this child."

Mr. Benjamin looked at Mr. Day in surprise.

But suddenly Mr. Day began to talk of something else. "You have parents living nearby?" he asked politely.

The other man answered quickly. "Oh, yes!" he said. "And wouldn't they just love a grandchild! They'd be tickled pink to have a little one to visit."

"I guess you don't see them much then," Mr. Day asked without great interest.

"Oh, we see them all right. Birthdays and that sort of thing. I've always made it a special point to do my duty. You know—honor your father and mother and all that," he said grandly. "I always send them something pretty fancy for their anniversary. Something really expensive!"

"And when was the last time you saw them?" Mr. Day asked, as if it wasn't very important.

The other man took time to think. "About New Year's last, I guess. Oh, no—we were pretty busy then. I guess it was before that."

A tight knot was growing bigger and bigger in Mr. Benjamin's chest. If the decision depended on how big a gift he had given his parents, well, he guessed he was out.

"And when did you last see your parents?" Mr. Day asked him.

Mr. Benjamin raised his head. "Yesterday," he mumbled. "I stopped by to give my mother a big red tomato." It sounded odd, he knew. He added quickly, "She loves tomatoes, and it was a specially nice one and . . ." his voice trailed off.

He guessed it was all over for him. A tomato didn't sound like much. It didn't sound like anything at all. He raised his head and met Mr. Day's gaze.

"It's just that she especially likes tomatoes," he said. Then he didn't know what more to say.

Mr. Day stood up. "What neither of you mentioned in your written application is what you would give this child besides his food and clothing and other things. We think that's important. Very important."

The man who looked like Mr. Benjamin scratched his head. "What do you mean?" he asked.

"The love a father will give his child can be judged by the honor the father shows his own parents," Mr. Day said carefully.

"I gave them a television set!" the other man said quickly.

Mr. Day nodded. He turned to Mr. Benjamin. He said kindly, "Mr Benjamin, would you mind waiting in the other room for a moment?"

Slowly Mr. Benjamin went into the other room. He sat there staring at the floor. He didn't know what he was going to tell Margaret.

"A television set," he mumbled as Mr. Day came in.

Mr. Day nodded. "A good dutiful gift," he said. "Even generous. But how can it compare with a gift of love?" He stood there smiling at Mr. Benjamin.

Mr. Benjamin's mouth fell open. "A big red tomato?" he said, not sure he was hearing right.

Mr. Day said, "A gift of honor!"

Mr. Benjamin began to smile, too.

"A man who honors his parents is sure to be a good father to his own child," Mr. Day said softly.

But Mr. Benjamin hardly heard him. He was thinking of what he had to tell Margaret, and his grin stretched all the way across his face.

· VI ·

You Shall Not Murder

· VI ·

You Shall Not Murder

Everybody was quiet. Everybody was still. The people listened to the Sixth Commandment. Clearly it did not mean that people shouldn't kill chickens and cows and other animals to eat because people have to eat to live. The commandment was against killing without need. That was murder.

Then people began to discuss the Sixth Commandment with one another and understood that it was not about death. It was about life.

Life was what made them breathe. It made their hearts beat. It made them feel and think. But no one could really say exactly what it was.

"Life is good," one Israelite said softly.

They remembered they had been told how God had made the world and called it good. And how God had created life and called that very good.

"Life is good!" The Israelites repeated, one after the other.

And then they began to understand what the Sixth Commandment was telling them. It meant that life is good. It is good above everything else. That is why you must value it.

You must protect life and treasure it, appreciate it and make the most of it. Not only your life, the commandment said, but the lives of all others. For every life is a world, God was saying, like God's world.

The Israelites breathed deeply, feeling the breath of life in their bodies. Life was good. They smiled, thinking that now they knew what the Sixth Commandment meant.

Then they heard a sound of thunder. It boomed like a warning over their heads.

It reminded them that the Sixth Commandment said something more. It said no one shall take away in anger a life that God had given in love. No one shall murder.

THE SIXTH COMMANDMENT

His Name Was Chaim

One day a stranger rode his horse into a little town. Tied to his belt was a bag. It clinked with gold pieces when he jumped off his horse.

"Good afternoon, stranger," called a townsman. "Where are you headed?"

The stranger didn't bother to answer. He had a few questions of his own to ask.

"Who is the bravest fellow hereabouts?" he asked the tavern keeper.

"Who has more ambition than he has gold?" he asked the barber.

"Who can keep a silent tongue in his head when necessary, yet talk himself into good favor?" he asked the baker.

It was a very small village, and everywhere he went the answer was the same.

"Chaim," they said. "It's Chaim you're looking for. He's a hard worker. He'll do almost anything for a dollar. He has one eye on the prettiest girl in the village and the other on a piece of the finest land hereabouts. He sings with the best of them in the evening. But he's up before the sun every morning to say his prayers. He's a good lad, that Chaim."

The stranger frowned. "A *good* lad?"

"And ambitious," said the barber. "He's the most ambitious young man around here."

The stranger smiled. "Tell me," he said, "where can I find him?"

"Who knows?" said the tavern keeper. "One day he is here, one day he is there. He is not one to stay in the same place very long. Not when there is work to be done."

"And where is here and where is there?" the stranger asked. He seemed very pleased.

"*Here* is the little synagogue on the corner, where he dusts the *bimah* and sweeps the schoolrooms. And *there* is the little farmhouse on the other side of the river."

The tavern keeper came out to shout after the traveler. "Watch the little bridge," he called. "It's a shaky one!"

The stranger nodded and rode through the village. The bridge was a very shaky one. To cross it, he slid off his horse and walked, leading the horse behind him. The tiny bridge spanned a deep river. Great rocks choked the river, and the water swirled around them. The stranger shivered and held on tightly to the railing.

Soon he reached the little farmhouse. He looked at it with interest. It was neat, stout, and well kept, but to his mind there wasn't much there worth keeping. He smiled contentedly to himself as he tied his horse to the fence post and rapped on the door.

"Who is there?" asked a voice from within.

The stranger did not bother to reply. He knocked again.

The door was flung open, and standing in the doorway was a young man so tall, so strong, and with eyes so clear and blue that the stranger stepped back in surprise.

"Chaim?" he asked. "You are Chaim?"

"I am Chaim," was the answer. "Who are you?"

The stranger smiled. "It is better that you do not know my name if you are the one I'm looking for."

Chaim looked curiously at the stranger. "All right, Mr. No-name," he said. "Come in." When the stranger had sat down, Chaim said, "Tell me, why do you think I am the man you are looking for?"

The stranger looked around the room. Everything was neat and everything was clean, but luxurious it was not.

"Because I have what you want," he replied.

"And what is it that I want?" asked Chaim.

"That is easy to see. You want a beautiful girl for a wife. And you want that good rich land I rode through for a farm. You want a fine house to put your wife into and more land to build it on."

Chaim laughed. "Are you a fortune-teller?" he asked. "One of those fellows who travels around promising little for much?"

The stranger laughed, too. "I am not a fortune-teller," he said, "but it is about a fortune I have come to see you."

"Mine?" said the young man, making a joke.

"Yours," said the stranger. "If you want it, that is."

Chaim looked at him. "Who would not want a fortune, sir?" he said lightly, but his eyes began to gleam.

The stranger drew his chair close. "I have with me a bag of gold," he said. "It will be yours if you do something for me."

Chaim leaned forward eagerly. "What is that?"

"Kill a man."

Chaim rose. His chair fell back onto the floor. Suddenly he laughed. "It's a joke!" he said. "A fine joke, sir. Now tell me what you came for and let me get on with my work."

But the stranger did not laugh with him. "It is no joke," he said.

Chaim stared at his visitor. The laughter left his face. "I cannot kill a man," he said. "Not for all the gold in the world. I cannot kill anyone. Not a dog in the street or even the ant that fell into my soup last night."

The visitor looked at him impatiently. "Come, come," he said. "You are an ambitious lad. I know that. And it is a simple enough thing to do." He pushed the sack of gold toward him.

Chaim opened the door. He picked up the sack of gold and threw it out the doorway. "Good-bye," he said. "You are only a fortune-teller after all. You want a lot for a little. All the gold in the world is not worth as much as one life." Then he grinned at his visitor. "If you don't believe me, just ask the man whose life it is."

"Bah!" said the stranger. He picked up the sack of gold. Mounting his horse, he pulled angrily at the reins. The horse reared up, turned around, and broke into a fast gallop.

"The bridge is shaky!" shouted Chaim and closed the door.

A little later he heard a strange noise in the yard. Opening the door, he saw the traveler's horse running around wildly, riderless.

"The bridge!" thought Chaim. He jumped on his own horse and raced to the shaky bridge. It was still standing, but a rail had broken away. Looking below, Chaim saw his visitor clinging to a rock. Chaim threw off his coat and jumped into the wild water.

"It is too late," shouted the desperate man.

But Chaim paid no attention. He tried again and again to reach the man. And again and again he was thrown back by the surge of the river.

"I'm afraid you can't," gasped the stranger, and his hands began to slip from the rock.

"I can!" shouted Chaim. "I will!"

Slowly he dragged the man up to the bank.

"Are you all right?" Chaim asked, when he could breathe again.

"Yes," was the answer. "Yes, I am all right." He turned to stare at Chaim.

"There's one thing I don't understand," he said. "A little while ago you refused a fortune in gold because a life was too valuable. Yet now you almost threw your own life away for nothing."

Chaim took a deep breath. "True," he said. "And I'll tell you why. Every time God creates a man or a woman, it is as though God has created a whole new world. Each and every life is like a world, you see. Me, murder?" He shook his head. "If I destroyed one person, it would be the same to God as if I had destroyed the whole world."

"But you almost destroyed your own life to save mine," said the stranger. He still couldn't understand.

Chaim smiled. "The way God counts, saving a life is the same as saving a whole world, too."

With a grin, the young man named Chaim climbed on his horse and whistled all the way home.

· VII ·

You Shall Not Be Unfaithful to Your Wife or Husband

·VII·

You Shall Not Be Unfaithful
to Your Wife or Husband

When the Israelites heard these words, husbands and wives moved closer together. The commandment was reminding them that marriage is a holy vow.

A marriage tells everyone in the world that two people have made a promise to each other to be faithful in body, word, and deed, the commandment said. And to those who listened very hard, it said much more: It said that marriage is God's blessing for happiness; it said that marriage is a partnership in which faithfulness, love, and understanding are shared responsibilities.

As they listened to the words of the Seventh Commandment, husbands and wives nodded. They were thinking of how both troubles and joys are shared in marriage. By sharing pain, each partner suffered only half as much. And by sharing joy, the partners doubled their happiness.

But there were many who heard in God's words a stern warning. Marriage makes a man and woman one in God's eyes, and neither husband nor wife must do anything to break that holy bond.

THE SEVENTH COMMANDMENT

The Promise

In a town long ago lived a young man who believed there was very little he did not know. Being very much in love and ready for marriage, he took to heart all the advice he had ever heard (although some was good advice and some was not). He was told that a husband's word is law. He was told that marriage is holy. He was told that marriage is a promise. But no one told him what a marriage really is.

Sitting at his wedding feast with his new wedding ring gleaming on his finger, he gazed at his bride with satisfaction. Afterward, he led her to his house and instructed his servants to do whatever she asked.

At the first Sabbath evening meal with his wife, they lit the candles together, drank the wine, and broke the bread. She called him her king, and he called her his queen. He couldn't help congratulating himself on having made such a perfect marriage.

The next morning he said to his wife, "You must promise me that nothing will ever interfere with our welcoming every Sabbath together." His wife laughed at his serious face and promised. Although she loved him very much, she thought her young husband was often foolish and sometimes hasty.

Every Friday afternoon he came home with flowers in his arms and a smile on his face. The table was set with a white cloth, candles, and wine glasses; the soup was simmering on the stove; and best of all, his wife was waiting to greet him.

One Friday when he arrived home, he saw the table set and smelled the soup simmering, but his wife was nowhere to be seen. He frowned.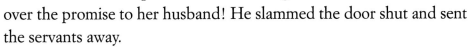

Suddenly there was a tap on the door. Opening it, he saw an old woman. "Your wife bid me tell you that she will be late for supper tonight. She is helping my neighbor birth her goat," she said and hobbled off.

A goat? The husband frowned some more. How dare his wife place the care of a goat over the promise to her husband! He slammed the door shut and sent the servants away.

As the hours passed, the husband became angrier and angrier. He paced up and down, from one end of the house to the other. Images of the uneaten Sabbath meal arose before his eyes and made his stomach rumble. He remembered how beautiful his wife had looked in the candlelight, but he hardened his heart against her. He reminded himself that she had broken her promise.

Making a quick decision, he rushed to the door and locked it. Then he went upstairs to bed. Although he soon heard knocking and tapping, he covered his ears with his pillow and went to sleep.

The next morning he went to the rabbi and announced that his wife had broken a promise and his marriage was over. Thoughtfully the rabbi gazed at the foolish young man. "Since your marriage began with a feast, let it end with a feast," the rabbi advised. The young husband then went home, where he found his wife waiting at the door, having spent the night at her father's house.

When he announced his decision without looking at her, she nodded and, without speaking, went to the kitchen to instruct the servants. That evening they sat down to a great feast with much food and wine. Halfway through dinner, feeling righteous and wanting to show that he was the most charitable of men, he said in a shaky voice, "Choose anything you desire in my home and take it with you when you return to your father's house."

"Thank you," she replied and filled his glass again. She kept filling it again and again until his hand could no longer hold the glass, his eyes closed, and his head fell on the table.

When he was in a deep sleep, she beckoned to the servants and said to them, "Pick him up and carry him to my father's house."

At midnight the husband woke up and, seeing nothing familiar around him, asked, "Where am I?"

"You are in my father's house," his wife replied.

He sat up. "What am I doing in your father's house?"

"Did you not say to me last night, 'Choose anything you desire in my home and take it with you when you return to your father's

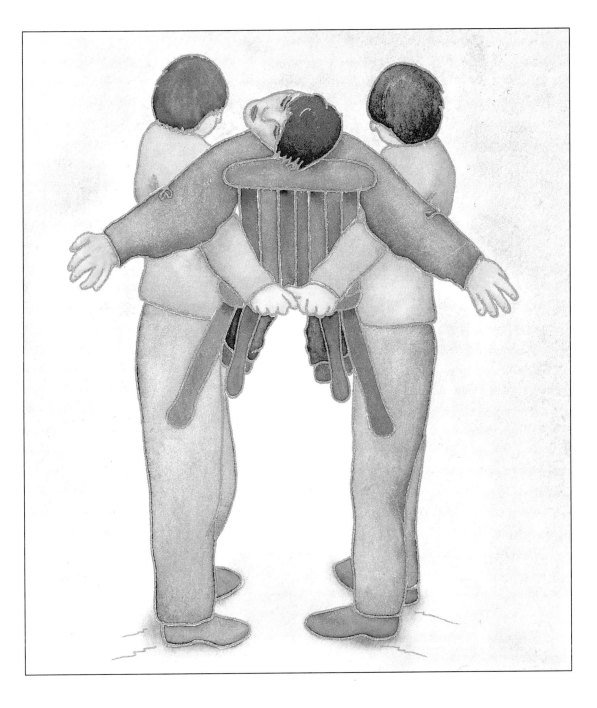

house'? There is nothing in the world I care for more than you."

And the foolish husband kissed his faithful wife. Together they returned to their home and from that day on, he was never quite so foolish again.

· VIII ·

You Shall Not Steal

· VIII ·

You Shall Not Steal

You shall not steal. How simple the Eighth Commandment sounded!

"Go on to the next commandment," some of the Israelites said to Moses. They didn't think this commandment could mean anything more. But Moses didn't go on to the next commandment. He waited until the little words had been heard deeply in all their hearts.

Taking something that belongs to someone else is stealing. Everyone knew that. When you stole something, you were punished. Slaves who took what was not theirs were whipped by their masters.

Thinking about this, the Israelites felt something strange and new. They had been thinking of themselves as slaves. Slaves are responsible to their masters. But the Israelites were their own masters now. They were free people.

"Free!" someone called out, thinking aloud.

As they thought about it, they could see that a free person has even greater burdens than a slave. For free persons must be responsible to themselves for whatever they do. They must be their own masters. They must tell themselves what to do. By doing what is right, they please themselves, and that is the way to please God.

The Eighth Commandment really meant that free men and women must respect one another and respect what belongs to others.

YOU SHALL NOT STEAL. It was strange how big the words sounded when their meaning became clear.

THE EIGHTH COMMANDMENT

The Reward

Once there was a very clever young man who owned only the clothes on his back and the smile on his face.

One day, in the court of King Solomon, he met an old artist who was looking for an apprentice.

"I need someone to learn my craft," the old man said. "If you promise to work hard, I will teach you all I know."

The young man shrugged. "Why not?" he said. But he had no intention of working very hard. His head was full of plans of how to earn money without doing any work at all.

Luckily for him, the old man was so honest and so busy that it did not occur to him that his clever young apprentice was paying no attention to the careful instructions he gave him.

News of the old painter's young apprentice soon reached the ears of the king, who was very wise and very kind. The king was pleased to hear that his old friend had found someone who would help him with the work he loved.

He called the two before him. "You must each paint my portrait," he said, and with a nod to the apprentice, he added, "Each must be exactly like the other." For the king knew that young people learn by copying their elders.

The old artist smiled. Never before had the king wanted a portrait of himself. To be chosen to paint one was a great honor. And what a splendid opportunity for his young apprentice, he thought.

"I will do my best, O King," he said, and he meant it.

But the young man, who was very clever, saw a way to become rich doing no work at all. He said, "But my king! A portrait to do you honor should be painted in gold and silver, with rubies and sapphires!" He shrugged his shoulders sadly. "We are but poor craftsmen. Where would we get such magnificent materials?"

"I do not expect you to make a king's likeness out of ordinary materials," the king said. "Whatever you need you shall have, both of you. Now go and get ready, and come back tomorrow. I will sit every afternoon for you until the portraits are finished."

The clever young man said quickly, "But you must not ask to see the portraits until they are completed."

To the old artist the young man's words seemed exceedingly wise.

"Agreed!" said the king.

So every day the king sat for his portrait. Every day the old artist worked with eager eyes and hands. And every day the clever young man went through the motions, as if he, too, were painting the king's portrait. But his canvas was blank, and he thought only of the rubies and pearls and diamonds that lay before him.

Pretending to measure the paint, he measured instead fine gold dust, enough to fill the pockets of his shirt. He dropped a ruby under his tongue when he licked his paintbrush to a fine point, and every afternoon he walked away from the palace with a pearl in the toe of his shoe. After the old man had fallen asleep, the young apprentice spent his nights lining his clothes with secret pockets. He carried his treasure with him wherever he went.

Each day the old artist's portrait came closer to being finished, and each day the canvas upon which the young man worked remained blank.

The young man planned carefully. He would stay, stealing all he could, until the last day but one, and on that day he would disappear. Poof! Just like that.

Unfortunately for him, it did not happen just like that. One day—three days too early—the old artist laid down his brush and said joyfully, "It is done!"

The young man looked up in surprise. Quickly he hid his blank canvas under a cover of velvet.

"You are finished, too, of course!" the king said. He rose and stretched.

"Of course!" the young man said, thinking fast. But of course he wasn't.

"Now I have a surprise for you," the king said. He clapped his hands.

Into the room came two of the king's servants. They carried two golden tubs, two large bars of sweet-smelling soap, and two great soft towels. Behind them came more servants with underclothes of silk, trousers of velvet, and shirts of the finest satin.

"You will be my guests at dinner," the king announced. "And after dinner, I will view the finished portraits!"

The old artist looked at the warm water in the tubs and at the fine clothes. He smiled with pleasure.

The young man frowned. In his secret pockets a fortune was hidden. He hesitated a moment too long, however, for two husky young servants quickly stripped him of his work clothes, rolled them into a ball, jewels and all, and carried them off.

The young apprentice sat in the tub and frowned at the water. What was he to do? He stared at the blue water around him. He studied his face reflected there, and a clever plan came to him. Suddenly he saw how he could deceive the king and save himself.

He allowed himself to be dressed in the fine clothes. When he was ready, he bowed to the king and asked him one small favor.

"O King," he said, "may I hang the portraits with my own hands? Only then will I know they are properly ready for the eyes of the king."

The king was much pleased. "As soon as our feast is over," he said, "you may take the portraits into my chamber and hang them as you think they should be hung."

The clever young man smiled brightly. Directly after dinner he did as he had planned. He took two gold frames and placed in one the portrait of the king that the old artist had so lovingly painted. In the other he fitted only a mirror, which he had taken from an empty room.

With much skill he placed the likeness of the king high on one side of the king's chamber. Opposite it he hung the framed mirror. He hung it in such a way that it reflected exactly the portrait of the king painted by the old artist. Anyone looking would see two portraits exactly the same, down to the last detail. He chuckled to himself.

When the king arrived, he walked first to the real portrait, and he raised his head to study it. "Magnificent!" he cried. "This is truly a work of art!"

The old artist smiled with pride.

Then the king turned and raised his eyes to the portrait that was really a mirror on the opposite wall. He looked at it closely. "Amazing!" he said.

The clever young man almost laughed out loud. Truly, the mirror on the wall seemed to be a portrait of equal beauty.

The king led the two artists to his treasure room.

"I thank you," he said to the old man and placed before him a large bag of gold.

The young man could hardly wait his turn. He congratulated himself on his cleverness and eagerly stepped forward to receive his reward.

"Wait!" the king commanded.

Startled, the clever man stepped back.

Next to the bag of gold, the very wise king had placed a mirror. "This is your reward," the king said, pointing to the reflection of the gold in the mirror.

And that is all it was.

· IX ·

You Shall Not Tell False Tales About Your Neighbor

You Shall Not Tell False Tales About Your Neighbor

At the words of the Ninth Commandment, many made a wry face. Repeating idle gossip and spreading rumors was what some of them had done many times without thinking. For it didn't seem as if just talk could hurt people much.

"When people tell false stories about their neighbors, they are stealing," an old man said wisely. "They are stealing their neighbors' good name."

Many looked at him in surprise. They had not thought about it in that way at all.

They began remembering how their people had become slaves in Egypt. The Israelites had lived happily in Egypt for many years until a cruel Pharaoh became ruler. He did not like the strangers in his land. He thought there were too many of them. He whispered to his people, "The Israelites are enemies. They must be kept down!"

"Oh!" said one Israelite, and "Oh!" said another. For they remembered how those false words had helped Pharaoh turn his people against the Israelites and make slaves of them.

With eyes wide open, the people who had found freedom considered the Ninth Commandment. In it, God was telling the Israelites that all people must beware of the words they speak about others, for words could hurt as much as weapons.

All of them began to shake their heads in agreement, and some shouted, "We hear!"

THE NINTH COMMANDMENT

The Gossip

Once there was a woman who talked so much about her neighbors that they all went to the rabbi to complain.

"She tells everyone that I eat cake instead of bread!" complained one woman, whose pudgy face was pink with distress. "I only said I'd like to; I didn't say I did. But she goes around telling everybody I do!"

"She says I'm too stingy to take a deep breath," said another.

"Every time she sees me, she tells me how nice I look. But to everyone else she says I look terrible for my age!" said another.

And another complained, "She's always telling people what a good cook I am. She tells everybody I am so good that I can make rancid butter taste like manna!"

"Is that bad?" asked the rabbi. It seemed to him to be a very good thing to be able to do.

"But she makes everybody think that I buy only the poorest-quality ingredients for my fine baking. And it is not true. I buy only the best!"

"I see," said the rabbi. "Yes, I see."

After he had heard all the complaints, he sent for the woman to come see him.

"Why do you make up stories about your neighbors?" he asked her.

She laughed, a pleased little laugh. "I don't really make up stories," she said. "I just tell them a little bigger than they really are."

"You see nothing wrong in that?" the rabbi asked.

She shrugged. "Most of the time it's just the plain truth, dressed up a little."

"And the other times?"

The woman laughed nervously at the rabbi's simple question. "Well, the other times, it's almost the truth, " she admitted.

The rabbi frowned.

"Anyway," she explained, "it's only talk."

Thoughtfully the rabbi looked at her. "Perhaps you are right," he said, agreeably enough.

The gossip smiled. "After all, Rabbi," she said, "what's talk? It isn't as if I can't take back what I say."

The rabbi only nodded. He folded his arms and spoke of other things.

As the woman was about to leave, the rabbi said, "I wonder if you would do something for me."

"Of course," she answered quickly. She leaned toward him. "I'm really not a mean person, Rabbi. I'll be glad to do anything I can for you."

He arose, went over to the couch in the corner, and picked up a plump pillow. Handing it to her, he said, "Take this pillow to the town square."

A little surprised, she tucked it under her arm. It was fine and full, packed tight with soft feathers.

"When you get to the town square, I want you to tear it open and shake out the feathers," the rabbi told her.

"Tear it open!" she said. "You mean—tear it open?"

The rabbi nodded. "Please do this for me," he said, "and afterward return here."

The woman shrugged. It occurred to her that perhaps their rabbi was getting a little old. But she carried the pillow, as he asked her, to the center of the town. As she walked, she smiled to herself. Tomorrow she would have a delicious story to tell the butcher. She would say that perhaps their rabbi could bear watching, that there were queer things going on in his head. Perhaps he was getting a little foolish. That's what she would say. She smiled, thinking of the stir she would cause with her words.

Soon she reached the town square. There she did just what the rabbi had asked her. She tore the pillow open and let the feathers fly. The light breeze in the town square blew off her hat and floated the feathers up and away. She ran after her hat and plopped it back on her

head. She could hardly wait to get home to tell her neighbors about the silly thing the rabbi had asked her to do.

When she returned to the rabbi's house, she told him that she had done exactly as he had asked.

"Fine!" said the rabbi.

"Oh, it made quite a show!" she said gaily. "The wind picked up the feathers and blew them all away!"

The rabbi nodded. He seemed pleased. He handed her a basket. "And now," he said, "please go back to the square and gather them all up again."

The woman gasped. "But that is impossible!" she said.

"Ah!" said the rabbi. "In the same way, it is impossible for you to take back all the unkind things you have said about others."

With that, he led her to the door and gently closed it behind her.

· X ·

You Shall Not Want
What Belongs
to Your Neighbor

· X ·

You Shall Not Want What
Belongs to Your Neighbor

The Israelites thought about the words of the last commandment.

The other commandments told the Israelites what they must not forget, what they must not do, and what they must not say. The Tenth Commandment tells them what they must not want.

They must not want anything that already belonged to someone else and that they could not honestly get for themselves, the Tenth Commandment said.

No matter how much they wanted something, they must not let their desire turn into envy. Envy keeps people from seeing and keeps them from thinking until they cannot tell the difference between what is right and what is wrong.

In the Tenth Commandment, God was reminding them that people must think as well as feel. "Do not let your feelings do all your thinking for you," God was saying in this commandment.

Suddenly the Israelites understood something they had not understood before. If they did not envy, they would not steal, they would not murder, and they would not be unfaithful.

God had separated a person's deeds, thoughts, words, and feelings into parts. The commandments showed them how to put these parts together in the right way. Every commandment was part of every other commandment. They all belonged together.

With a great sigh, the Israelites accepted the Tenth Commandment. At last they knew how free people should live.

THE TENTH COMMANDMENT

The Peach, the Pitcher, and the Fur Coat

Once there was an old man who lived in a big house. Although he was not rich, he had three prized possessions—a peach tree, a silver pitcher, and a coat with a fur lining.

Every day he would sit at the window of his house and look at the tree growing in his yard. Only one peach grew on it.

In the house across the yard lived a woman with her son. This boy, too, spent his days at his window. His head was almost always bent over his desk. But as summer wore on, it seemed to the old man that the student was gazing out the window more often than he was looking at his books.

One day, to his surprise, he did not see the boy's face at the window. But as the days went by, he soon forgot about the boy. The peach grew ripe. It was time to pick it.

As he stood below the tree admiring the fruit, the woman from next door called to him.

"Good sir," she said, "have you a moment?"

"Of course," he replied. "I was just about to pick my peach and eat it."

The woman said. "Dear sir, I have a son who is sick—because of you."

"Me?" said the old man. "Why me?"

"Well, not you, exactly," she said. "I mean because of that peach you are about to eat. You see, my son sits at the window overlooking your tree. Now his yearning for that peach has made him ill."

"You don't say!" said the old man in surprise. "Well, tell him to get out of bed for I will be happy to give it to him."

"Oh, thank you!" the woman said.

So the old man picked his beautiful peach and gave it away.

The weeks went by and summer turned to fall. Each day the old man sat at his window looking out upon his yard. And each day the boy sat at his desk with his eyes on his books.

As the days became colder, the old man fixed himself a little cocoa in the silver pitcher. Then he would sit, sip the hot cocoa, and stare out at the bare garden.

Soon he began to notice that the young man across the way was looking more at the silver pitcher than at the books before him. Shortly after that, the old man could no longer see the boy's head in

the window. "That's funny," he thought. But as day followed day, he almost forgot about his neighbor. Then one day his front doorbell rang.

"Good day!" he said warmly as he opened the door. It was the woman from next door.

"Oh dear," she said. "Oh dear, oh dear. It is not a good day at all. It is a very bad day at my house."

"What is the trouble?" the old man asked.

"It is my son again, sir. He's taken to his bed, although I can't say what the trouble is. He keeps talking about a silver pitcher." She looked at the silver pitcher on the table.

"It is really of no great value," the old man said. "But I've had it for such a long time. I hardly think . . ."

The woman wrung her hands. "He is so young, my dear sir. And the young have so far to go."

"True," said the old man, but he frowned.

She said timidly, "He says that if only he could touch the beautiful silver pitcher and pretend it was his own, he would be able to get up and go on with his work."

The old man went over to his table and picked up the silver pitcher.

"Your son shall have it," he said generously. "And not just for a day. For always. You tell him it is a gift from me."

After the woman had carried his precious silver pitcher away, the old man stood in the middle of his room and sighed. The young have so much to learn, he thought, and he put away his disappointment.

Every day, as usual, he sat at his window looking out. But he no longer had the peach to look upon, nor even the taste of the peach to remember. And he no longer had the silver pitcher shining warmly at his elbow.

Nevertheless, he was content with what he did have. There was his fur-lined coat, which he laid around his shoulders every day. It pleased him to see the student's head so earnestly bent over his books. Perhaps he will be a great doctor, the old man comforted himself, or a scientist. With his eyes closed, he dozed under the warmth of the fur-lined coat.

But there came another day when he no longer saw the young man's head at the window. And a few days later, he heard a knock at the door.

"Come in," he called. He stood up, holding the coat so that it would not slip off his thin shoulders.

The door opened and there stood his neighbor.

"Oh, it's you," he said. He waited. Suddenly he knew what was coming.

Timidly she said, "My son . . ."

He nodded grimly.

She twisted her hands together. "He cannot sleep. He cannot study. He dreams all night long. He longs for a fur coat." The good woman began to cry. "He says he will surely die if he cannot have a coat of fur. Oh please, sir, can you help him?"

Thoughtfully he answered, "I think perhaps I can."

The old man wrapped his coat closely around him and followed the woman across the yard and up the stairs to the boy's room.

True enough, the boy looked near death. His eyes were dark holes in his face. But the old man pretended not to notice how the boy looked at his coat.

"I have come to save your life," he said and smiled thinly at the boy's cry of delight. But he was in no hurry to take off his coat. He picked up a book that lay open on the desk. He looked at the papers lying there. Then he grunted and sat down.

"You are a smart boy," he said. "You have a good head. It should take you where you want to go, if you will let it."

The boy nodded impatiently. His eyes were fastened on the fur-lined coat.

"Long ago, my father told me a story," said the old man. "And I am going to tell it to you."

• • •

Once there was a snake. One day the snake was coiled happily in his favorite spot when his tail thumped him from behind.

"Who's that?" asked the head sleepily.

"It's me," said the tail, "your tail."

The head opened his eyes and looked at the tail. "What's the matter?" he said. "Why do you thrash around like that?"

"I'm thrashing around because it seems to me that you've been leading us around long enough. It's my turn."

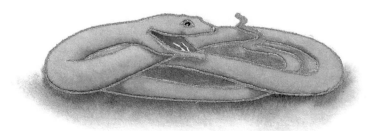

"You?" said the head. "But you cannot think. How can you lead us anywhere?"

"Maybe I can't think," said the tail, "but I can feel. And I feel very deeply. I feel it is my turn to be the leader for a change."

"All right," said the sleepy head. "If you feel you must, you must, I suppose. Go ahead."

Well, the tail could feel all right, but he couldn't see and he couldn't think. So he began dragging the snake into all sorts of places. Through a swamp and a nasty blackberry bramble. Up a tree of thorns and down again. The poor snake's head bumped along behind. His eyes were scratched and his fangs were at the wrong end when he needed them most. Finally, the poor head had been bounced around so much that he scarcely had anything left to think with. And since the tail never did have anything to think with from the start, he led the head into a bad spot and WHAM! That was the end of the snake—both head and tail.

◆ ◆ ◆

The boy looked down at his feet.

"Like the snake," the old man said, "a man is born with a part for thinking and a part for feeling. When the head is doing its job, this works out pretty well. But when a man lets his feelings do all his thinking for him, then maybe he's wearing a tail where his head should be."

With that, the old man got up and said, "Good day," and, clasping his fur coat closely around him, he went home.

We Will Hear

The Israelites took the Ten Commandments into their hearts and the responsibilities that went with them onto their shoulders.

They said, *Na'aseh venishma*! "We will do and we will hear!"

Around these commandments, they built their way of life. It became their religion. Today this religion is called Judaism, and the people who live according to it are Jews.

It is your religion. This Judaism of yours is an inheritance that has come to you from almost 4,000 years ago. It belongs to you. But it is not something that you *have*. It is something that you *do*.

It is something that you can lose but cannot give away; something that you can keep but cannot hide.

And you keep it by *doing*.

The Ten Commandments are the pillars upon which Judaism rests. The Law of the Jewish people, the Torah, started with the Ten Commandments, and almost all of it is concerned with *doing*. "Do not do to others what you do not want them to do to you."

These words seem so simple that almost everyone knows them by heart, and anyone can say them standing on one foot.

Many have wondered how a people without a homeland for 2,000 years outlived so many nations that were stronger. Perhaps it is because the words of the Torah are exceedingly wise, and the Torah is the heart of Judaism. Perhaps it is because the Jewish people live in strength as long as that heart beats, no matter what happens.

And perhaps Judaism became one of the strong religions of the world because the Ten Commandments hold the secret of peace on earth.

What the Ten Commandments really say is, respect God and respect life. Respect your parents, your sisters and brothers, your husband or wife, your servants, your animals, your neighbors, and the stranger within your gates, and respect all that belongs to them.

Furthermore, they say, respect yourself, through rest and work, through doing and understanding.

Judaism helps you live your life the best way you can—for yourself, for your family, and for all humankind.

This is SOMETHING IMPORTANT.

Learn to say again in the words of your ancestors who stood at the foot of Mount Sinai, *Na'aseh venishma*! "We will do and we will hear!" Then the world will be a better place because you live in it.

♦ ♦ ♦ ♦ ♦

The Ten Commandments

ONE

I am your God who took you out of the land of Egypt,
out of the house of slavery.

TWO

You shall have no other gods besides Me.

You shall not make idols of anything in the sky,
on the land, or in the waters.
You shall not bow down to them or serve them.

THREE

You shall not use God's name falsely.

FOUR

Remember the Sabbath day and keep it holy.

Six days you shall labor and do all your work, but the seventh day is a Sabbath of your God: You shall not do any work—you, your son or daughter, your servants, your animals, or the stranger who is in your home. For in six days God made heaven and earth and sea, and all that is in them, and rested on the seventh day; therefore, God blessed the Sabbath day and made it holy.

FIVE

Honor your father and your mother.

SIX

You shall not murder.

SEVEN

You shall not be unfaithful to your wife or husband.

EIGHT

You shall not steal.

NINE

You shall not tell false tales about your neighbor.

TEN

You shall not want what belongs to your neighbor.

You shall not want your neighbor's house,
your neighbor's spouse, your neighbor's servant,
or anything that is your neighbor's.

ASL Classic